Will the Reds Win?

by Rachel Russ
Illustrated by Bill Ledger

OXFORD
UNIVERSITY PRESS

In this story ...

Jin

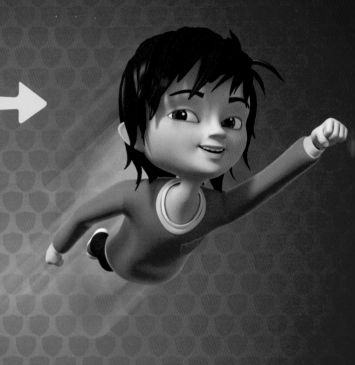

Jin can lift off!

Pip

Ben

2

Jin gets a red vest.

The red vests bat.
Ben hits it.

Ben is fast and gets seven runs.

Pip bats next.

Pip jogs.
Pip gets six runs.

Jin bats next.

Jin cannot hit it.

Jin is fed up.

The black vests will bat next.

It is a hit!

Jin jets up.

Jin gets it.

The reds win!

Retell the story ...

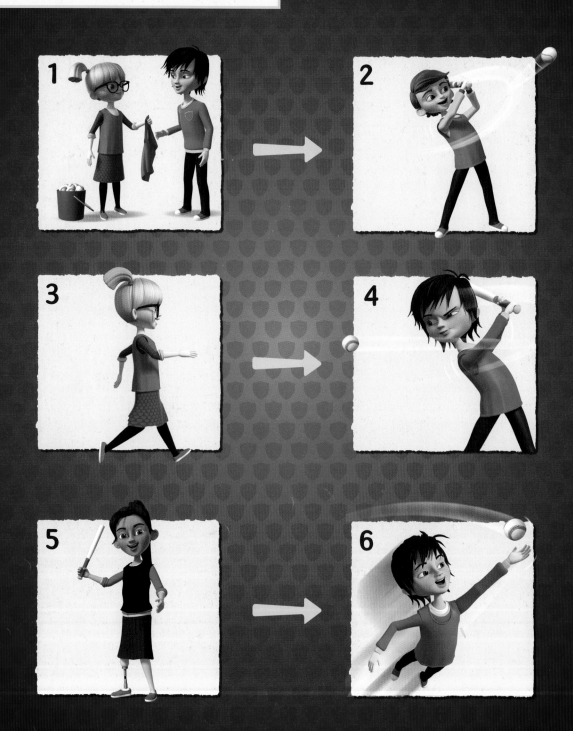